Show me your garden and I shall tell you who you are.

— ALFRED AUSTIN (1857–1929)
English writer

Marsh Marigolds

The Gardener's Notebook

Gardening is a craft, a science, and an art. To practice it well requires the enthusiasm of the true amateur and the understanding of the true student.

— LOUISE AND JAMES BUSH-BROWN, b. 1900, 1903
American horticulturists

The great challenge for the garden designer is not to make the garden look natural, but to make the garden so that the people in it will feel natural.

— LAWRENCE HALPRIN, b. 1900
American gardener

Iris

A weed is no more than a flower in disguise,
Which is seen at through at once, if love give a man eyes.

— JAMES RUSSELL LOWELL (1819–1891)
American poet

Malope

To work in the garden is to be brought into contact with the elements of botany, geography, ecology, genetics, chemistry and entomology—not to mention ornithology, bacteriology and meteorology—and interest may develop in any of these directions.

— ALICE M. COATS, b. 1899
American horticulturist

Originally, the word "weeds" was we'ods, and it was the Anglo-Saxon name for all herbs and small plants . . . to past generations of men, all plants were regarded with respect.

— AUDREY WYNNE HATFIELD, b. 1950
American naturalist

*What is a weed? A plant whose virtues
have not yet been discovered.*

— RALPH WALDO EMERSON (1803–1882)
American writer

Thistle

A garden is a thing of beauty and a job forever.

— ANONYMOUS

One to rot and one to grow,
One for the pigeon, one for the crow.

— OLD ENGLISH PLANTING RHYME

Impatiens

How miraculous that growing on my own little plot of land are plants that can turn the dead soil into a hundred flavours as different as horseradish and thyme, smells ranging from stinkhorn to lavender.

— JOHN SEYMOUR, b. 1914
English naturalist

Grass

Grass is the forgiveness of Nature.

— THOMAS CARLYLE (1795–1881)
English historian

Nature does not complete things. She is chaotic. Man must finish, and he does so by making a garden and building a wall.

— ROBERT FROST (1875–1963)
American poet

Cactus

But a little garden, the littler the better, is your richest chance for happiness and success.

— REGINALD FARRER, b. 1899
English writer

The best fertilizer for a piece of land is the footprints of its owner.

— LYNDON B. JOHNSON (1908–1973)
American President

Once we become interested in the progress of the plants in our care, their development becomes a part of the rhythm of our own lives and we are refreshed by it.

Hollyhock

When there's new growth bursting out all over, everything fresh, green, and flourishing, the plants are little rockets of success going off every time you look at them.

— JACQUELINE HERITEAU, b. 1925
American writer

Flowers are words which even a baby may understand.

— ARTHUR C. COXE, b. 1900
English writer

Peony

Every garden is a chore sometimes, but no real garden
is nothing but a chore.

— NANCY GRASBY, b. 1918
American writer

Probably more pests can be controlled in an armchair in front of a February fire with a garden notebook and a seed catalog than can ever be knocked out in hand-to-hand combat in the garden.

— NEELY TURNER, b. 1900
American entomologist

Squash

But gardens are places in which men come home again, in which they realize,
that "Art itself is nature."

— TERRY COMITO, b. 1935
English historian

Streptocarpus

Gardens cannot be considered in detachment
from the people who made them.

— DEREK CLIFFORD, b. 1913
American historian

A killing frost devastates the heart as well as the garden.

— ELEANOR PERENYI, b. 1920
Hungarian-born writer

Christmas Cactus

*Even if something is left undone, everyone must take time
to sit still and watch the leaves turn.*

— ELIZABETH LAWRENCE, b. 1934
American writer

It is worth any amount of effort to be able to see your house through the arch of a tree.

— THOMAS D. CHURCH, b. 1918
American writer

Daffodil

The word "garden" is at root the same as the word "yard." It means an enclosure.

— DEREK CLIFFORD, b. 1913
American historian

All gardens are the product of leisure. It is no good looking for gardens in a society which needs all its energies to survive.

— DEREK CLIFFORD, b. 1913
American historian

Snowdrops

A city garden, especially of one who has no other, ought to be planted and ornamented with all possible care.

— MARCUS PORCIUS CATO (234–149 B.C.)
Roman statesman

How can one help shivering with delight when one's hot fingers close around the stem of a live flower, cool from the shade and stiff with newborn vigor?

— COLETTE (1873–1954)
French writer

Orchid

The strange thing which I have experienced with flower scents, and indeed with all other scents, is that they only recall pleasant memories.

— THEODORE A. STEPHENS, b. 1907
English editor

I don't think you can separate a person from his work, which is why I say care is what makes the garden. It also makes the gardener.

— JAMES JANKOWIAK, b. 1942
American gardener

Coleus

*I think the reason most of us do like houseplants
is simply that they are alive.*

— JERRY BAKER, b. 1932
American author

I don't know whether nice people tend to grow roses
or growing roses makes people nice.

— ROLAND A. BROWNE, b. 1939
American professor

There, with her baskets and spades and clippers, and wearing her funny boyish shoes and with the sunborn sweat soaking her eyes, she is a part of the sky and earth, possibly a not too significant part, but a part.

— TRUMAN CAPOTE, b. 1924
American writer

Clematis

If you really want to draw close to your garden, you must remember first of all that you are dealing with a being that lives and dies; like the human body, with its poor flesh, its illnesses at times repugnant. One must not always see it dressed up for a ball, manicured and immaculate.

— FERNAND LEQUENNE, b. 1935
French attorney and writer

To take a spade or spading fork on a crisp fall day and without undue haste or backbreaking effort to turn over slice after slice of sweet-smelling earth can bring rich rewards to the gardener who fully understands just what he is accomplishing.

— T. H. EVERETT, b. 1900
American landscaper

Veronica

He who plants a garden, plants happiness.

— CHINESE PROVERB

Lily-of-the-Valley

A flower is the most eligible object in the world.

— DONITA FERGUSON, b. 1892
American gardener

My good hoe as it bites the ground revenges my wrongs, and I have less lust to bite my enemies. In smoothing the rough hillocks, I smoothe my temper.

— RALPH WALDO EMERSON (1803–1882)
American philosopher and essayist

Lettuce

Love of flowers and vegetables is not enough to make a good gardener. He must also hate weeds.

— EUGENE P. BERTIN, b. 1920
American horticulturist

Unlike most other works of art, a garden requires of its owner something more than mere appreciation.

— LOUISE AND JAMES BUSH-BROWN, b. 1900, 1903
American horticulturists

You fight dandelions all weekend, and late Monday afternoon there they are, pert as all get out, in full and gorgeous bloom, pretty as can be, thriving as only dandelions can in the face of adversity.

— HAL BORLAND, b. 1921
American journalist

Grape Hyacinth

Earth laughs in flowers.

— RALPH WALDO EMERSON (1803–1882)
American writer

Gazania

To dig and delve in nice clean dirt
Can do a mortal little hurt.

— JOHN KENDRICK BANGS (1862–1922)
American writer

Horticulturally, the month of May is opening night, Homecoming, and Graduation Day all rolled into one.

— TAM MOSSMAN, b. 1945
American editor

I'm still devoted to the garden . . . although an old man, I am but a young gardener.

— THOMAS JEFFERSON (1743–1826)
American President

Dusty

Miller

As gardens are to the Japanese a vital part of living, they must not only express the spirit and essence of nature, but also the dignity of man.

— SAMUEL NEWSOM, b. 1890
English historian

Gardening can become a kind of disease. It infects you; you cannot escape it. When you go visiting, your eyes rove about the garden; you interrupt the serious cocktail drinking because of an irresistible impulse to get up and pull a weed.

— LEWIS GANNIT (1898–1953)
American writer

Lotus

There's something soothing about firming seeds in the soil and tending plants under the glass of your greenhouse while raindrops and snowflakes fall against the panes.

— GEORGE ABRAHAM, b. 1928
American gardener

Nicotiana

Apprentice yourself to nature. Not a day will pass without her opening a new and wondrous world of experience to learn from and enjoy.

— RICHARD W. LANGER, b. 1932
American writer

Eggplant

Tomatoes and squash never fail to reach maturity. You can spray them with acid, beat them with sticks and burn them; they love it.

— S. J. PERELMAN (1904–1980)
American humorist

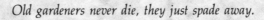

Old gardeners never die, they just spade away.

— MURIEL COX, b. 1910
American gardener

Tulips

Nothing is more pleasant to the Eye
than greene Grasse kept finely shorn.

— FRANCIS BACON (1561–1626)
English philosopher

It may be argued further that real beauty is neither in garden nor landscape,
but in the relation of both to the individual, that what we are seeing is not only
a scenic setting for pool and fountain and parterre, but a background for life.

— SIR GEORGE SITWELL (1860–1943)
English writer

The joy of being able to cut flowers freely, lavishly, to decorate the house and to give to friends is an end that justifies a lot of gardening effort.

— T. H. EVERETT, b. 1900
American landscaper

Marigolds

Hundreds, yes, literally hundreds, had come out in a single night; the green bushes bowed down as though they had been visited by archangels.

— KATHERINE MANSFIELD (1888–1923)
English writer

Pansy

*One of the healthiest ways to gamble is with a spade
and a package of garden seeds.*

— DAN BENNETT, b. 1940
American journalist

In the garden, more grows than the gardener sows.

— SPANISH PROVERB

Who loves a garden still his Eden keeps.

— AMOS BRONSON ALCOTT (1799–1888)
American educator

Poppy

When I was most tired, particularly after a hot safari in the dry, dusty plains, I always found relaxation and refreshment in my garden. Lone female that I was, this was my special world of beauty: these were my changing styles and my fashion parade.

— OSA JOHNSON (1894–1953)
Swedish adventurer

African Violet

Love of flowers and all things green and growing is with many men and women a passion so strong that it often seems to be a sort of primal instinct, coming down through generation after generation.

— HELENA RUTHERFORD ELY (1850–1907)
American gardener

To create a little flower is the labour of ages.

— WILLIAM BLAKE (1757–1827)
English poet and mystic

They'd lived through all the heat and noise and stench of summertime, and now each widely opened flower was like a triumphant cry, "We will, we will make a seed before we die."

— HARRIETTE ARNOW, b. 1908
American writer

Echeveria

The most noteworthy thing about gardeners is that they are always optimistic, always enterprising, and never satisfied. They always look forward to doing better than they have ever done before.

— VITA SACKVILLE-WEST (1892–1962)
English writer

Only man deliberately rearranges the setting he lives in simply because he prefers the look of it.

— NAN FAIRBROTHER, b. 1940
American horticulturist

The works of a person that builds begin immediately to decay; while those of him who plants begin directly to improve. In this, planting promises a more lasting pleasure than building.

— WILLIAM SHENSTONE (1714–1763)
English poet

Carpathian
Harebells

An old woman in blue jeans, lugging pails of sand or humus, handling fork or spade, may be an edifying sight but it is hardly the picture of leisured dignity one would like to present to the neighbors.

— BUNKER HOLLINGSWORTH, b. 1900
American writer

He who sows the ground with care and diligence acquires a greater stock of religious merit than he could gain by the repetition of ten thousand prayers.

— ZOROASTER (630/618–553/541 B.C.)
Persian theologian

English Daisy

Statice

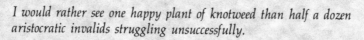

I would rather see one happy plant of knotweed than half a dozen aristocratic invalids struggling unsuccessfully.

— MARGUERITE JAMES, b. 1910
English writer

Gardening shouldn't be a grim business. If you've forgotten that, it's time you learned a lesson from your children.

— RICHARD NICHOLLS, b. 1949
American writer

The Amen! of Nature is always a flower.

— OLIVER WENDELL HOLMES (1809–1894)
American author

Columbine

A plant is like a self-willed man, out of whom we can obtain all which we desire, if we will only treat him his own way.

— JOHANN WOLFGANG VON GOETHE (1749–1832)
German poet

Rose is a rose is a rose is a rose.

— GERTRUDE STEIN (1874–1946)
American writer

One of the most attractive things about flowers is their beautiful reserve.

— HENRY DAVID THOREAU (1817–1862)
American essayist

No two gardens are the same. No two days
are the same in one garden.

— HUGH JOHNSON, b. 1939
American horticulturist

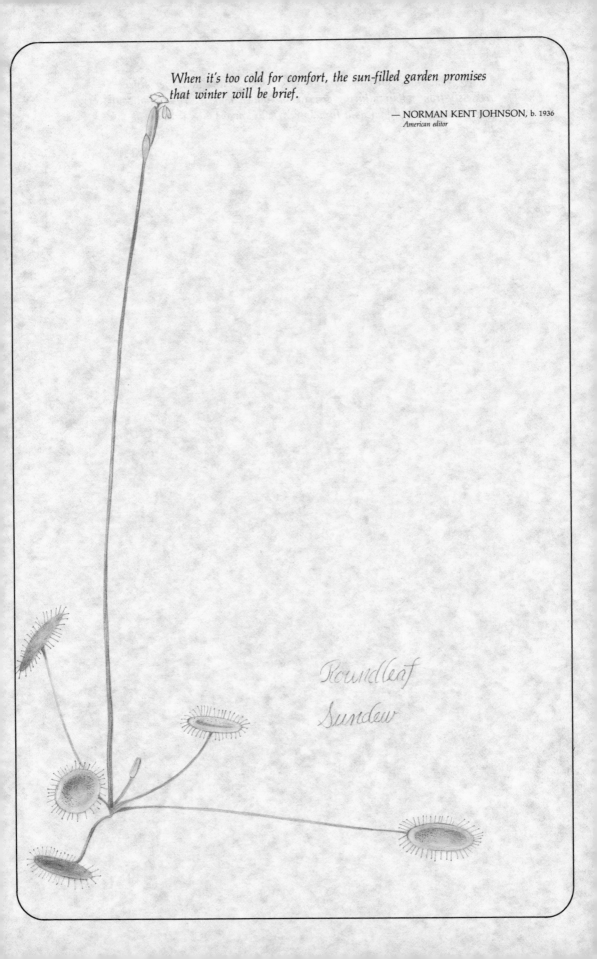

When it's too cold for comfort, the sun-filled garden promises
that winter will be brief.

— NORMAN KENT JOHNSON, b. 1936
American editor

Roundleaf
Sundew

I have grown wise, after many years of gardening, and no longer order recklessly from wildly alluring descriptions which make every annual sound easy to grow and as brilliant as a film star. I now know that gardening is not like that.

— VITA SACKVILLE-WEST (1892–1962)
English writer

Early gardens are planted on the pray-as-you-sow plan.

— EDYTHE SOPER, b. 1912
English naturalist

Crocus

Oh, Adam was a gardener, and God who made him sees
That half a proper gardener's work is done upon his knees.

— RUDYARD KIPLING (1865–1935)
English writer

What a man needs in gardening is a cast-iron back, with a hinge in it.

— CHARLES DUDLEY WARNER (1829–1900)
American writer

Strawberry

Making a garden, no matter how simple, is a creative endeavor and it should relate to the person who owns it and be in some way a conscious expression of himself.

— NANCY GRASBY, b. 1912
English horticulturist

Sinningia

One of the best things about a garden, large or small, is that it is never finished. It is a continual experiment.

— MARGERY BIANCO, b. 1944
American horticulturist

Morning glory

I believe a leaf of grass is no less than the journey-work of the stars.

— WALT WHITMAN (1819–1892)
American poet

In gardening, one's staunchest ally is the natural lust for life each plant has, that strong current which surges through everything that grows.

— JEAN HERSEY, b. 1903
American gardener

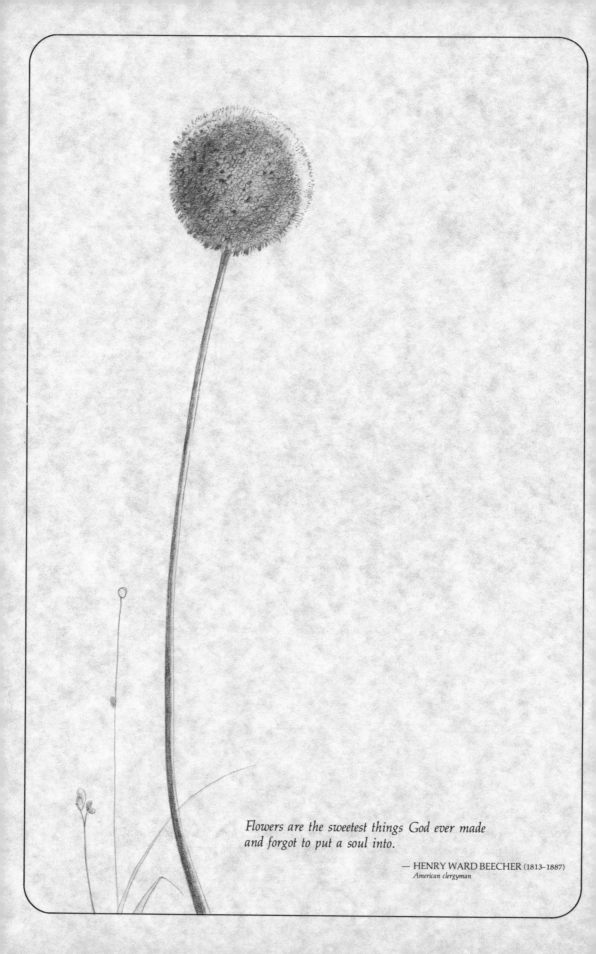

*Flowers are the sweetest things God ever made
and forgot to put a soul into.*

— HENRY WARD BEECHER (1813–1887)
American clergyman

The realization that, much as we love them, flowers are not the basic component of our outdoor areas is the first step toward creating satisfying and effective plantings of them.

— NANCY RUZECKA SMITH, b. 1921
American gardener

Allium

The best place to seek God is in a garden. You can dig for him there.

— GEORGE BERNARD SHAW (1856–1950)
English playwright and essayist

Orchid

*There is one thing that you will find practically impossible
to carry into your own greenhouse and that is tension.*

— CHARLES H. POTTER, b. 1927
American gardener

The kiss of the sun for pardon,
The song of the birds for mirth —
One is nearer God's heart in a garden
Than anywhere else on earth.

— DOROTHY GURNEY (1858–1932)
American poet

Baby's
Breath

A garden is the one spot on earth where history does not assert itself.

— SIR EDMUND GOSSE (1849–1928)
English critic and writer

Hasta

It is apparent that no lifetime is long enough in which to explore the resources of a few square yards of ground.

— ALICE M. COATS, b. 1899
American horticulturist

The home gardener is part scientist, part artist, part philosopher, part plowman.
He modifies the climate around his home.

— JOHN R. WHITING, b. 1922
American writer

As every estate agent knows, a poor house in good surroundings will sell for a higher price than a better house in poor surroundings, and in a town they confidently ask 25 percent more rent for a flat with a view of a park than for an identical flat with no view.

— NAN FAIRBROTHER, b. 1940
American horticulturist

Fuchsia

A house without a garden is a house with no foundation at all, a house subject to all the hazards of life. But a garden with no house is a garden with no soul.

— FERNAND LEQUENNE, b. 1935
French attorney and writer

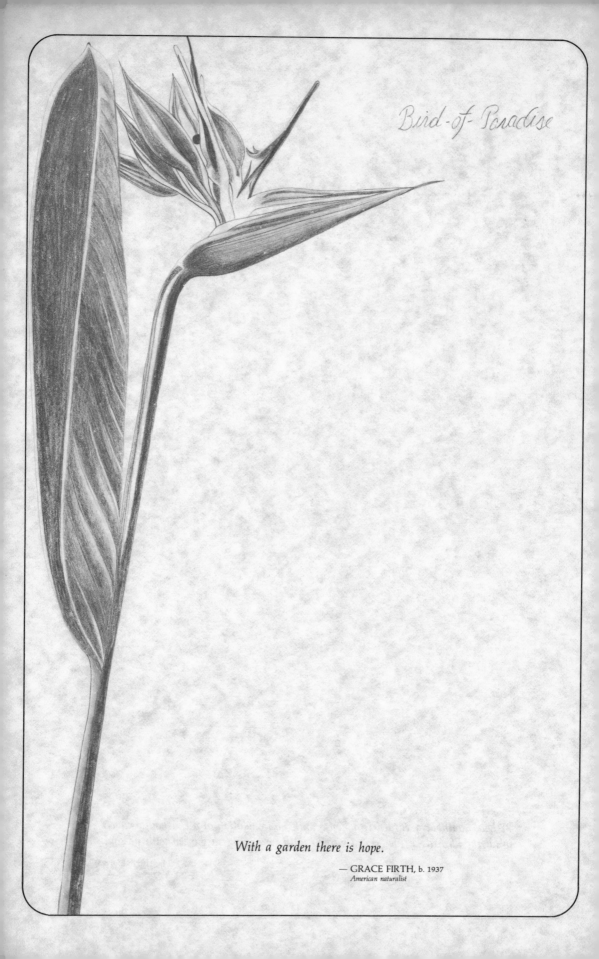

Bird-of-Paradise

With a garden there is hope.

— GRACE FIRTH, b. 1937
American naturalist

595 ISBN: 0-89471-204-